Blastoff! Discovery launches a new mission: reading to learn. Filled with facts and features, each book offers you an exciting new world to explore!

This edition first published in 2020 by Bellwether Media, Inc.

No part of this publication may be reproduced in whole or in part without written permission of the publisher. For information regarding permission, write to Bellwether Media, Inc., Attention: Permissions Department, 6012 Blue Circle Drive, Minnetonka, MN 55343.

Library of Congress Cataloging-in-Publication Data

LC record for Ghost Ships available at https://lccn.loc.gov/2019000969

Text copyright © 2020 by Bellwether Media, Inc. BLASTOFF! DISCOVERY and associated logos are trademarks and/or registered trademarks of Bellwether Media, Inc. SCHOLASTIC, CHILDREN'S PRESS, and associated logos are trademarks and/or registered trademarks of Scholastic Inc., 557 Broadway, New York, NY 10012.

Editor: Kate Moening   Designer: Andrea Schneider

Printed in the United States of America, North Mankato, MN.

TABLE OF CONTENTS

A Foggy Phantom	4
Haunted Waters	8
Strange Sightings	10
Searching for Phantoms	18
Blame the Weather	24
An Age-old Mystery	28
Glossary	30
To Learn More	31
Index	32

A FOGGY PHANTOM

Jackie and Lars stare out at the Atlantic Ocean. Thick clouds blanket the night sky. Dark water slaps the sides of their ship as they watch and wait. It is only their first night sailing around the coast of South Africa. But the **investigators** hope to glimpse the *Flying Dutchman*!

After four quiet hours, Jackie walks around the deck to stretch her legs. Suddenly she calls out from the other side of the ship. Lars grabs his **binoculars** and rushes over!

Jackie aims her video camera at a dim red light in the distance. It is moving closer. Lars watches through his binoculars as large sails cut through the mist. The sails look black and torn. Suddenly, they vanish. The red light blinks out, too.

Jackie and Lars race to check their **radar**. But it shows no ships nearby. As Jackie checks her camera, Lars wonders what he saw. Was it a trick of the light? Or did they just meet a ghost ship?

HAUNTED WATERS

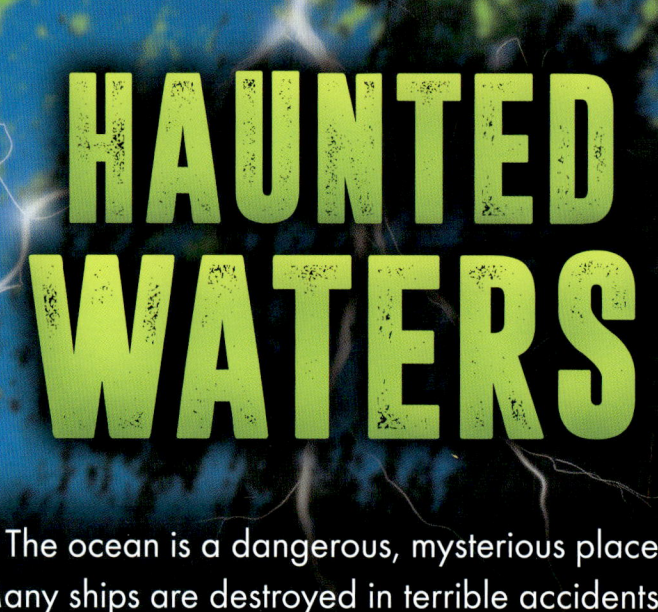

The ocean is a dangerous, mysterious place. Many ships are destroyed in terrible accidents or vanish without a trace. Some say the oceans are haunted by the **phantoms** of these ill-fated ships!

ONE CREEPY CRUISE

The ghost ship *Caleuche* is a famous legend in Chile. It is said to sail around Chiloé Island carrying the souls of those who have drowned. Witnesses say the *Caleuche* has red sails and shining white sides. They often hear music and laughter from its deck!

According to some **legends**, ghost ships bring the souls of sailors to the **afterlife**. Others say the ships are doomed to sail the seas forever. **Eyewitnesses** report ghost ships glowing or blazing with fire. Some say the ships fly through the air or sail beneath the waves.

STRANGE SIGHTINGS

Early ghost ships only had eyewitnesses for **evidence**. One was seen by a whole town! In 1647, the **New Haven colony** sent a trade ship to England. It never returned. Nearly two years later, witnesses watched a similar ship approach shore. It sailed through the air! Suddenly, the ship vanished. Many believed it was the trade ship's ghost.

A CURSED CAPTAIN

Phantom sailors haunt many old legends. In one popular tale, a Viking captain steals a magical ring from the gods. In return, they curse him to sail a black ship for all time!

Some phantoms appeared many times. In 1786, a fiery ship began haunting Canada's Northumberland **Strait**. Witnesses said it had burning white sails. They often heard gunfire. Over the years, dozens of people have seen it sail the strait.

Many eyewitnesses wrote about their encounters. One of the first writings about the *Flying Dutchman* appeared in 1795. George Barrington was a ship passenger when crew members saw the *Dutchman* during a storm. It quickly vanished! Barrington was a **skeptic**, but he included the sighting in a book.

replica of the *Flying Dutchman*

THE GREAT CHALEUR CHASE

Thousands have sighted Canada's Fireship of Chaleur Bay. In 1951, a magazine reported one appearance off the shore. A fishing company owner ordered his crew to catch the glowing phantom. They chased it across the bay before it disappeared!

USS Kennison

As sailing technology improved, ghost ships puzzled sailors in new ways. In 1942, the USS *Kennison* came across a strange, old ship. But radar showed nothing nearby. Five months later, crew members saw a similar ship. Again, their radar was silent. The ship vanished before their eyes!

Lake Superior

Eyewitness reports continued into the 21st century. In 2008, teenager Mathieu Giguere was visiting Canada's Tatamagouche Bay. The bay was frozen over. But Giguere saw a bright white and gold ship, clear as day. He believes it was the Ghost Ship of Northumberland Strait.

mirage

Sometimes, witnesses catch ghost ships on camera. In 2016, Jason Asselin was filming a rainbow over Lake Superior when he saw something shimmering far away. The strange shape disappeared after 30 minutes. Skeptics say it was a **mirage**. But Asselin remains unsure.

illustration of the Flying Dutchman

PROFILE: THE FLYING DUTCHMAN

Stories of the *Flying Dutchman* began around the 1600s. The huge black ship had ragged sails and a strange glow. It could fly over water or upside down! Sailors believed the *Dutchman* brought bad luck.

Early on July 11, 1881, thirteen people on the HMS *Bacchante* saw another ship approaching. The glowing red *Dutchman* soon disappeared. Only hours later, the first witness fell from the **mast** and died. Another crew member died soon after. Passenger Prince George V of Wales wrote about the event. But written reports are the only evidence the *Flying Dutchman* exists. Most skeptics believe it is a mirage.

CAPE OF GOOD HOPE, SOUTH AFRICA

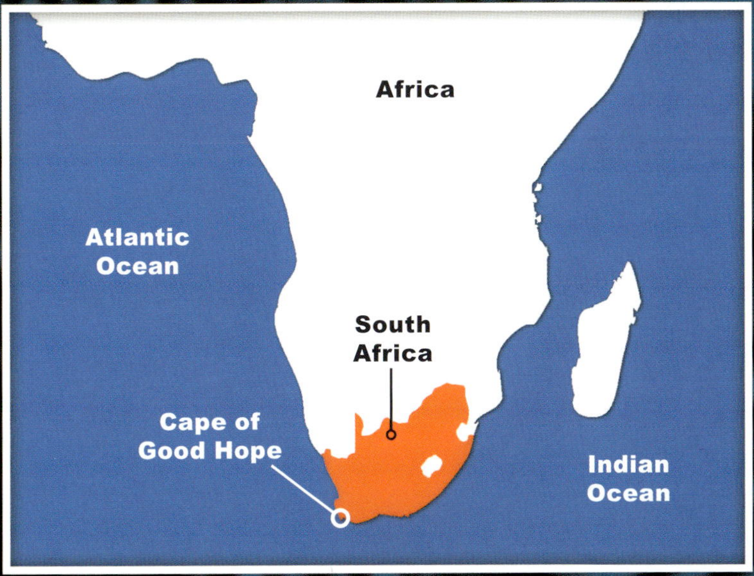

A FOOL'S ERRAND

The *Flying Dutchman* became famous with a story printed in 1821. A British magazine said the *Dutchman's* captain tried to sail past Africa's Cape of Good Hope during a terrible storm. For his foolishness, the captain was cursed to sail the seas forever.

SEARCHING FOR PHANTOMS

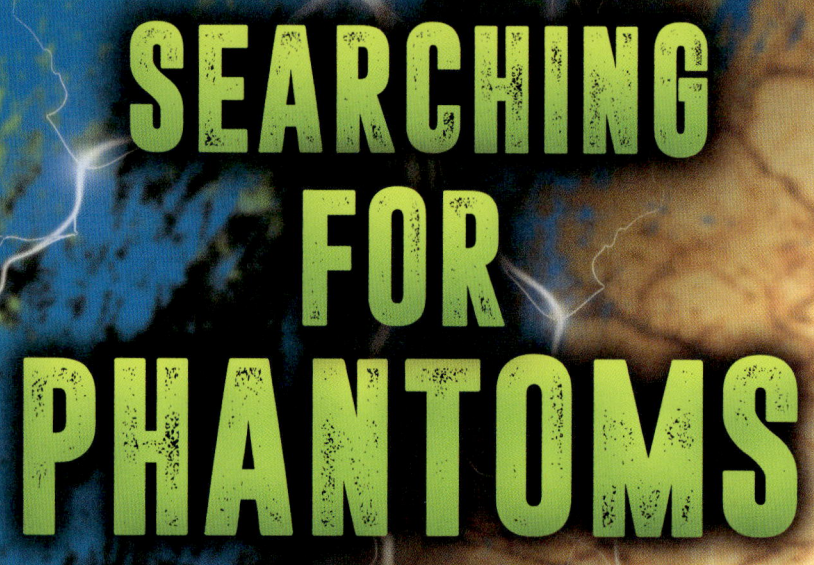

There are very few ghost ship hunters. But anyone can investigate if they have the right tools! A simple notebook is useful for logging important details of a case.

Phantom ships often appear in the same areas and follow the same paths. Investigators must research past sightings to be in the right place at the right time. Many ghost ships appear too far from shore to see. Investigators must sail to these locations on ships of their own.

INVESTIGATOR TOOLBOX

- notebook
- marine binoculars
- video camera
- radar
- automatic identification system

compass

telescope

binoculars

For centuries, sailors used **telescopes** and binoculars to observe ghost ships. Today's binoculars are extra powerful. **Marine** binoculars can withstand water and fog. Built-in **compasses** show investigators which direction an object is heading. Some binoculars even have **night vision**!

Cameras are important for recording live encounters. Photos and videos can be studied as evidence. But images can also be blurry. Many modern cameras have **image stabilization** to help take clear photos and videos.

SNEAKY SAILING

Automatic identification systems can sometimes be tricked. Ships sometimes turn their AIS off while traveling. These "hidden ships" may seem extra mysterious!

radar

automatic identification system

Rain, fog, or spooky mirages can make normal ships look ghostly. Tools like radar help separate real ships from phantoms. If a ship appears on radar, it is likely not a ghost.

Many ships also have an **automatic identification system** (AIS). A ship's AIS sends its name, speed, and location to other ships nearby. AIS receivers collect this information and display it on a screen. If a sighted ship does not match the AIS, it is worth investigating!

BLAME THE WEATHER

Skeptics point to simple reasons for ghost ship sightings. One popular argument is the fata morgana mirage. This mirage occurs when warm air meets cold air above the ocean. The temperature change can bend light rays. The rays hit the human eye at an angle, which makes objects look higher than they really are.

MORGAN'S MAGIC

The fata morgana mirage is named after Morgan le Fay, a character in many British legends. Le Fay was a powerful witch. In some tales, she used these mirages to trick sailors!

HOW A FATA MORGANA WORKS

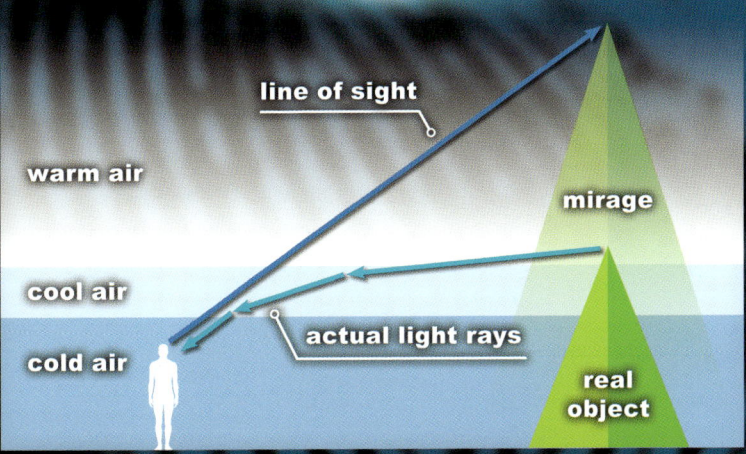

1. **Light rays travel from the object to your eyes.**

2. **Warm air rises and cold air sinks. The cold air bends light rays downward as they pass through.**

3. **To your eyes, it looks like the rays traveled in a straight path. This tells your brain the object is much higher up than it is.**

In a fata morgana, objects can appear huge and warped. Ships might look like they are flying or sailing upside down! The mirage can also bring into view ships that are already over the horizon.

Skeptics point out that heavy rain, fog, or snow can trick the eye. What looks like a ghost ship may really be rocks or shadows. Regular ships might look extra spooky.

Weather could also explain glowing ghost ships. Storms increase the amount of electricity in the air. At high levels, this electricity can create continuous sparks that glow bright blue or purple. These strange floating lights are called "Saint Elmo's fire." But people might mistake them for something ghostly!

AN AGE-OLD MYSTERY

Stories alone cannot prove ghost ships are real. Yet phantom ships continue to fascinate the world. They appear in books, movies, television shows, and even operas!

Most people are skeptics, and serious investigations are rare. Still, the open ocean remains full of mystery. Eyewitnesses report strange encounters to this day. Are they nothing more than old sailor stories? Or do ghost ships haunt much more than our legends?

SPOOKY STAMPS

In June 2014, Canada created a postage stamp featuring the Ghost Ship of Northumberland Strait. It was released on Friday the 13th!

GLOSSARY

afterlife—a place where people's souls may go after death

automatic identification system—a system used by ships to track the location of other ships

binoculars—a device used to look at things that are far away

compasses—devices used to find direction by means of a needle that always points north

evidence—information that helps prove or disprove something

eyewitnesses—people who see something happen firsthand

image stabilization—technology used in cameras to prevent blurry images when a camera is in motion

investigators—people who try to find out the facts about something in order to learn if or how it happened

legends—stories from the past that are believed by many people but not proven to be true

marine—of or relating to the sea

mast—a long pole that supports sails of a boat or ship

mirage—something that is seen and appears to be real but that is not actually there

New Haven colony—a small English colony that existed from 1643 to 1665, in what is now the state of Connecticut

night vision—technology that magnifies light coming in to allow people to see in the dark

phantoms—ghosts

radar—a system that uses radio waves to track and find objects

skeptic—a person who doubts something is true

strait—a narrow channel connecting two large bodies of water

telescopes—tube-shaped devices used to see things that are far away

TO LEARN MORE

AT THE LIBRARY

Gould, Jane H. *The Flying Dutchman*. New York, N.Y.: Powerkids Press, 2015.

Oachs, Emily Rose. *Ghosts*. Minneapolis, Minn.: Bellwether Media, 2019.

Roland, James. *Frightful Ghost Ships*. Minneapolis, Minn.: Lerner Publications, 2017.

ON THE WEB

FACTSURFER

Factsurfer.com gives you a safe, fun way to find more information.

1. Go to www.factsurfer.com.

2. Enter "ghost ships" into the search box and click 🔍.

3. Select your book cover to see a list of related web sites.

INDEX

afterlife, 9
Asselin, Jason, 15
Atlantic Ocean, 4, 17
automatic identification systems, 22, 23
Barrington, George, 12
binoculars, 4, 7, 21
Caleuche, 8
cameras, 7, 15, 21
Cape of Good Hope, 17
Chile, 8
compasses, 19, 21
England, 10, 17, 24
fata morgana, 24, 25
Fireship of Chaleur Bay, 12
Flying Dutchman, 4, 7, 12, 16-17
George V, Prince of Wales, 16
Giguere, Mathieu, 14
HMS *Bacchante*, 16
image stabilization, 21
Lake Superior, 14, 15

le Fay, Morgan, 24
legend, 8, 9, 10, 24, 28
mirage, 15, 16, 23, 24, 25
New Haven colony, 10
night vision, 20, 21
Northumberland Strait, Canada, 11, 14, 29
notebook, 18
radar, 7, 13, 22, 23
Saint Elmo's fire, 27
sightings, 10, 11, 12, 13, 14, 15, 16, 18, 24
skeptic, 12, 15, 16, 24, 26, 28
South Africa, 4, 17
Tatamagouche Bay, Canada, 14
telescopes, 21
tools, 4, 7, 13, 15, 18, 19, 20, 21, 22, 23
USS *Kennison*, 13
weather, 7, 12, 17, 21, 23, 26, 27

The images in this book are reproduced through the courtesy of: PLRANG ART, front cover (ship); Sasin Paraksa, front cover (skeleton); Kate Mur, pp. 2-3, 30-32; Spacedromedary, pp. 4-5 (ship); Eaum M, pp. 4-5 (ocean); FOTOGRIN, p. 5 (man); Elenarts, pp. 6-7 (ship); Lisa STrachan, pp. 6-7 (boat railing); Unholy Vault Designs, pp. 8-9 (boat); meunierd, pp. 8-9 (pirates); iurii, pp. 10-11; EmbraerSkyPilot/ Wiki Commons, pp. 12-13 (*Flying Dutchman*); Wiki Commons, p. 13 (USS *Kennison*); Wandering Introvert, pp. 14-15 (Lake Superior); simoncritchell, p. 15 (mirage); North Wind Picture Archives/ Alamy, p. 16; Pushish Images, pp. 18-19; Desing Projects, pp. 20-21 (ship); ArnuphapY, pp. 20-21 (ocean); hain.tarmann, p. 21 (telescope); Igor Kardasov, p. 21 (binoculars); Shahnewaz Mahmood, pp. 22-23; Digitalsignal, pp. 24-25; Xavier Roc Ayats, pp. 26-27; e71lena, pp. 28-29 (ship); Sergey Nivens, pp. 28-29 (ocean).